Inside a Radio Station

By Jeffrey B. Fuerst

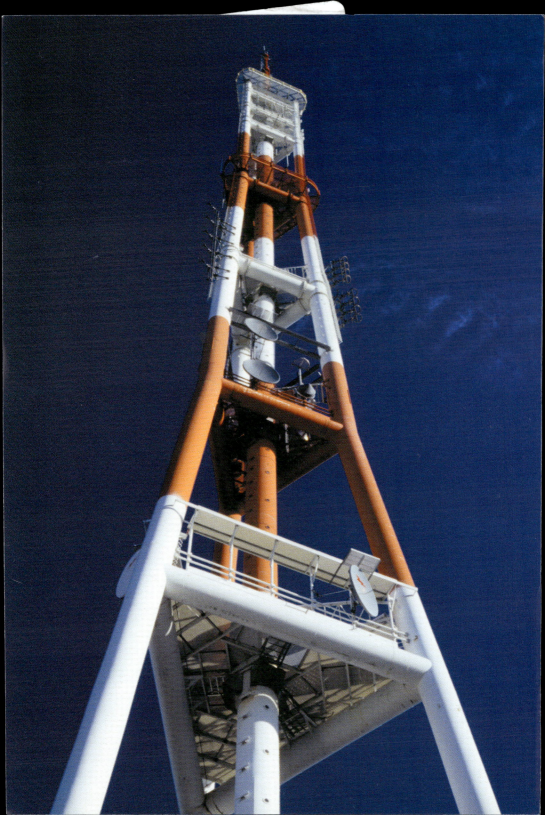

Contents

Radio's Many Voices 4
The Station 6
The Broadcast Studio 9
The Recording Studio 14
The Newsroom 17
The Equipment Room 20
Glossary 24

Radio's Many Voices

"It's seventy-two beautiful degrees here at K-X-Y-Z," says the radio announcer.

Skrickkk!

You fiddle with the radio, trying to find a good station.

"Top of the hour, time for the news…"

Skrickkk!

"And that was new music from the Trashcan Zombies, 'My Potato Only Has Eyes for You'…"

Skrickkk!

Turn on the radio and you can hear music, news, weather, and more anytime, anywhere.

But do you ever wonder who are the people behind radio's many voices? And how do these voices, sounds, and songs get to your radio? Step inside a radio station and find out!

Today's weather...
The Request Line is...

The Station

Welcome to station KXYZ! All radio stations in the United States are named using letters like this, called **call letters.** No two stations have the same call letters.

Many radio stations look just like office buildings on the outside. But inside there are rooms full of wires, microphones, computers, and people. They all help bring the sounds of radio to your ears.

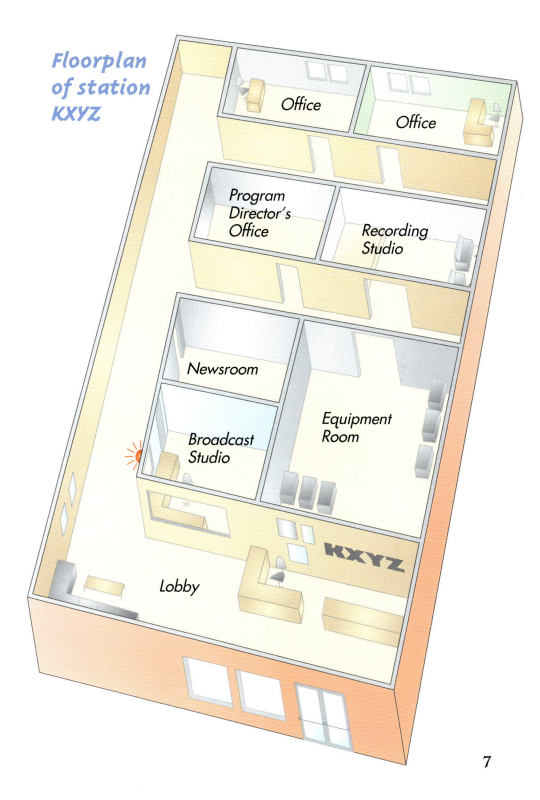

on the air

A light outside the studio flashes whenever someone is **on the air,** broadcasting a show.

Here's another tune...

The Broadcast Studio

"Here's another tune for all you veggie lovers," says the radio disc jockey, "'I'll Cry You a River If You Cut Me Some Onions.'"

The disc jockey, or DJ for short, is the host of this radio show. A DJ works in a small room called a **broadcast studio.** It is carpeted and lined with sound-absorbing materials. This is so outside noise won't get into the radio show, or **broadcast.**

DJs often have nicknames and say funny things. They want people to like them and listen to their show.

Between songs, the DJ talks into a microphone. Then the DJ presses a button labeled "Start/Next" to play another song. The song is stored in a computer. It can hold thousands of songs at a time.

The program director, or PD, picks the songs the DJs play each day. The PD also decides when commercials are played. The songs and commercials are listed on the computer in the **program log.**

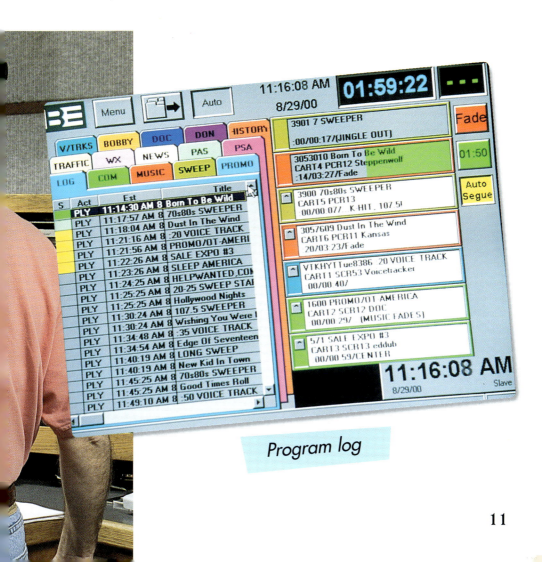

Program log

Program director

The PD of a music station is often a former disc jockey. The PD helps hire the DJs and tells them how to do a better job.

Before a song ends, the DJ checks the program log to find out what's up next. It might be another song, a newsbreak, or a commercial.

More after this from the International House of Pants...

The Recording Studio

Radio stations, like TV stations, get paid by companies to put commercials on their shows.

How to Make a Commercial

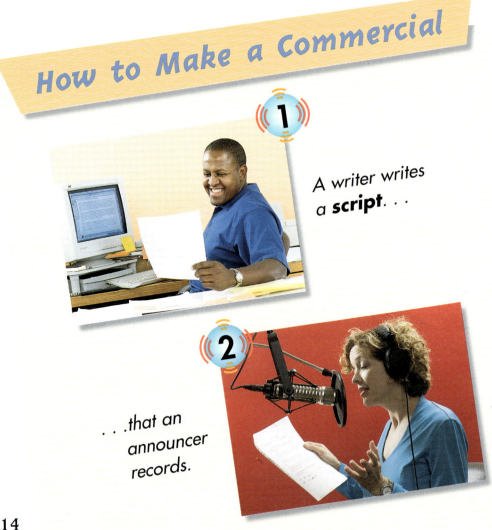

1. A writer writes a **script**...

2. ...that an announcer records.

Some commercials are made in the radio station's recording studio. It takes special equipment and lots of people working together to make just one commercial.

Meanwhile, an audio editor or the production director finds the right music and sound effects. Then the production director puts all the pieces together. This is called sound editing. He or she uses a special computer called a **digital audio workstation.**

"It's the top of the hour. Let's find out what's happening in the world."

DJs make sure the commercials go on at the right time. DJs make sure news reports go on at the right time, too. Sometimes, DJs give live news reports. Or sometimes, they introduce the news announcers.

 The Newsroom

People at radio stations wear many different hats. News announcers, especially at smaller stations, also research and write news stories.

To find stories, they read many newspapers every day.

They also can check a special computer. It shows up-to-the-minute news reports from around the world.

Sometimes, news announcers interview famous people on the phone and record their conversations. When broadcasting the news, announcers play a **sound bite** of the interview.

The Equipment Room

How do all the voices that start in the broadcast studio get to your radio many miles away? They travel through wires and machines that fill a whole room! An engineer checks every few hours to make sure everything is running smoothly.

An engineer

The equipment room is the heart of the radio station. From here, the voices are sent to a **transmitting antenna** and into the air. You hear them instantly on the radio in the car…by your bed…at the beach… almost anywhere!

KXYZ plays all hit songs all the time...

Circles of Sound

Have you ever tossed a pebble into a pond? Circular waves grow from the spot where it hits the water. A transmitting antenna works in a similar way. The transmitting antenna sends out invisible circles, or waves, of sound. Your radio catches these sound waves and then turns them into sounds you can hear.

Glossary

broadcast: A radio show; or to send out a radio show into the air.

broadcast studio: A soundproof room where radio shows are broadcast.

call letters: The letters (usually four) used in a radio station's name.

digital audio workstation: A special computer used for sound editing.

on the air: Broadcasting a live show.

program log: A daily record of what is broadcasted.

script: The written text of a radio show or a commercial.

sound bite: Part of a tape-recorded interview played on the air.

transmitting antenna: The tall metal tower that sends out radio waves.